Future Poet's Whispers of Real Desire Shared

FUTURE POET

authorHOUSE®

AuthorHouse™ UK Ltd.
500 Avebury Boulevard
Central Milton Keynes, MK9 2BE
www.authorhouse.co.uk
Phone: 08001974150

First published by AuthorHouse 1/14/2009

ISBN: 978-1-4389-4450-0 (sc)

Library of Congress Control Number: 2009900119

Printed in the United States of America
Bloomington, Indiana

This book is printed on acid-free paper.

This book is dedicated to my son

Kymani Peter Thierry Nelson

Contents

To the Reader

'To every thing there is a season, and a time to every purpose under the heaven:'
Ecclesiastes 3:1

The poems you'll read in this book may make you smile or even cry, bring back memories or provoke your inner thinking.

Either way, my intentions are that when you have finished reading this book, you will have felt moved, enlightened and empowered.

Much Love, Peace, & Guidance to you all

Bless

Future Poet

Acknowledgements

First and foremost I have to give thanks and praise to God for blessing me with this talent and the opportunity to share my words.

I thank my Mum and Dad, and my brother and sister, Karl and Kándis, for their individual support.

A special thank you goes to each member of my family:

Tianna for inspiring me, believing in me and for being my sister through high times of joy and low times of adversities!

Tishan for keeping me grounded and for being unique!

Sabrina for being in my life from day one and for keeping it genuinely real!

Darren (Boon) for being the No.1 supporter of my work and for attending every one of my poetry performances.

Chris for your straight talking, consistent motivation and for keeping me passionate about my work and overall creativity!

Deborah D for literally bringing back my enthusiasm and zest for life!

Dulani for mentoring me into realising my full potential and for showing me that my mind was 'mentally obese with knowledge' and the time had come to share it!

Joe for your encouragement and support and for stepping into my presence when you did!

Marlon G for your consistent support from the first day our paths crossed!

Randi for your introduction to the poem 'Time' and for your attentiveness, support and loyalty!

Wayne for the inspiration you have given me and for the confidence you have unknowingly stored within me!

A huge THANK YOU goes out to everyone who has knowingly and unknowingly inspired my writings in some way! I also thank those of you who have listened keenly to poems in progress and supported me at events. All of you have made a special contribution to my life and I sincerely thank you all!!!

Bless

Future Poet

Future Poet

Exhale

I exhale words of poetry
Through my heart and soul with my vibe
I exhale words of poetry
That relate to the reality of mankind's lives
I exhale words of poetry
To heal wounds that are not visual by sight
I exhale words of poetry
To help my own mind survive
I exhale words of poetry
Because it's my contribution to making the
world's wrongs right
I exhale words of poetry
Hoping that we can talk and not fight

My Temple

My temple is what holds me
It shows my identity
Which in turn is judged by others mentally
My mind controls the temple that beholds me
Its wisdom is of years before me
Sometimes I wonder if it's already made this journey
My temple is spiritually protected by the aura that surrounds me
Its skin is of Afro-Caribbean quality
Its flesh is made with the grace and charm of a lady
Its bones are built with pride, respect and dignity
The heart of my temple beats with love and a unique personality
The veins of my temple flow with strength inherited from ancestors before me
The breath of my temple exhales soulful words of poetry
My temple is only the shell that holds me
It's blessed with the beauty that God gave me
It presents me
Gives me identity
But when you see my temple don't think you see all of me
You're only seeing the shell that holds the inner me

My hair has come back home

I've never loved my hair
The way I love my hair now
I never really appreciated it
Western life had never taught me how
So within me I drew deep
And conditioned my life to a different place
I taught me how to love me
With God's help and my ancestors grace
I've allowed my hair's heritage to replace
The chemicals which tried to erase
It's beauty, its spirit, its charm
The creativity it can embrace
Locs I choose to wear
My inner conscience has chosen to bare
My hair's thickness, its naturalness
Its kink and its flare
And my hair now grows with strength
And with time my locs will gain length
While my inner pride repents
Against the wrong I've put my hair through
The things I did to it before
Now I'd never do
My hair now is where it belongs
I'd mistakenly lost my way before
But now I've found my route home
My hair, like me, has met its peace now
My hair has come back home

The War of Ambition

Right now I'm living in the trenches of a war

Between my heart and my senses
When it comes to my ambitions
I'm very defensive
Especially when negativity from others
Drenches… my soul
And tries to dishearten me from reaching my goal

"Only success can be the remedy that
Quenches the thirst
I have to be first
In all I do
Never the worst
Because a failure is not you"

A phrase I repeat daily
In order to fight through
The mental battle
The daily struggle
The animosity and trouble
That exists in the life I live
No matter how hard I try
I will never be rid
Of those who want to drown my dreams
With ifs, buts and maybes
Those who try to tell me
That as a poet I'll never make it

Pessimism has their aura imprisoned
While optimism has my aura
Relishing in its freedom
But with words I will beat them
Make them understand and learn
That the desire for what I yearn
Has a flame of passion that will forever burn

Life at a

Different

Angle

Time

"Everyday we're given 86400 seconds of what we refer to as time. This is my observation of this precious commodity."

Time is said to be a healer
And to make the heart grow fonder
Time is money
It is a journey through life
Time never stops running
And can never be stopped
But yours can
And when it does time itself will still be running
Time waits for no -one
When you think of time you're either on or you're late
But nothing runs according to the speed of time
Other than what has never been touched by mankind
Time is a dictation and definition of how we live
Time runs us and we live life unknown as to when
time itself will stop
Time brings experience and experience teaches
wisdom
Time is not to be wasted or to be reckoned with
It's to be appreciated
And to be used creatively, passionately and wisely

Time is life....

Music is...

Music is...
The beat of the drum
The equalized rhythm of the treble and bass
It intensifies your soul
Regardless of your musical taste

Music is...
The pleasurable sound of stretched strings
Be it by strumming or plucking
A guitar's acoustic or bass strings
Or drawing a bow across a cello bass or violin

Music is...
The strength of breath used to create
The soulful sensual sound of a saxophone
Trombone, clarinet, or trumpet
The sound of the blues from these Woodwinds
Is the sound that you will get

Music is...
The synchronized tapping of fingers
On keys of a forte or mezzo piano
Accompanied by the vocals of a contralto or soprano
Collaborated with the harmonized sounds of
percussion
Giving your ears nothing more than the entertaining
sound of musical perfection

Music deepens the soul
It stimulates the mind
Music reaches the parts mankind can't
Music is every note, every stanza, every key
Music is in you and music is in me

Clipped Wings

I feel trapped in my own thoughts
Locked away in my mind
Confined to a space where each square metre has
been physically covered
I have an unusual urgency to free myself
To untie my motivation
To release all my energy and frustrations
To make good everything that is bad
My mental feels weakened and my presence
unwanted
My physical paralysed
Like a wild bird with clipped wings is how I feel when
I'm trapped in my mind

Me

I've lost my identity
I want to find me
I want to be me
I'm confused by my mirror image's reality
The me I see
Is not the me that is me
My conscience is trapped in a whirlwind of frustration
It tells me I'm happy because I smile
But the expression doesn't make me
My paranoia tries to protect me
From me unwillingly hurting me
But my spirit is forcing me
To accept the adult changes within me
I want my soul to push through the real me
Release me into this matrix society
Unchain the locks of my insecurity
Allow me to be me
But not the me that you see
Just the me that is within me

Bredren Jokes

You want me to help you
But how can I help you
If you won't help you, to help you
You want me to hear you
Listen to your problems and reason with you
But how can I hear you
If you won't allow you to hear you

You want me to aid and assist you
Relieve some of the everyday pressures of life
From upon and within you
But yet everyday you bring a new issue before you
I just don't understand you
You want me to do all this for you
But then what do you do

You want me to help you
Hear you, aid you and assist you
So what …do you also want me to live your life for
you
Because that I won't do
Can't do and shan't do

Why should I step in your shoe?
When you won't step out to see you from my view!
I refuse to do for you
The actions you won't
I refuse to do for you
The simple tasks that you don't
I refuse to do for you
If you can't help you
To help me, to help you

Buil' Him

I have the urge to unwind
I looked at my friend
And pulled him out of his bed
I held him in my hands
I caressed him I stroked him
Gently... I...folded him
And licked him
Making sure my tongue covered each corner of his
fold
I pulled him apart softly
I need to, I want to, I have to go that one step further

You see I have a good friend
He is almost everyone's good friend
He sat there watching
Waiting for his turn
So I touched him
Teasingly I unclothed him
I could smell him through his clothes
He smelt good, his aura feels good, and he is good
Subconsciously he knows and I know he wants to
take me higher
Higher than I've ever been before
He wants me to feel him deep inside of me

And so I began to prepare him physically
I crumbled him, doing so passionately
I worked him between my fingers sensuously
I lay him in the fold of my other friend
And adjusted their bodies into the correct position
I then proceeded to roll them
Making sure each roll was done tightly and carefully

I have now produced the perfect man
I have prepared him, caressed him and built him
And now I will end him
You see my intention from the beginning was always
to simply...
Smoke him
And so I did!

Food for thought

How old are you?
What age is your mind?
Compared to that of your body
What age were you
When you became your own authority
Have you moved forward from your teens?
Are you yet to achieve
Any of your aspirations or dreams
Of experiencing your life's time to its extreme

Have you kept faith and believed?
Have you been true to yourself and lived clean?
Where has your mind, body and soul been?
Who have you shared your love and yourself with?

Who has been your guiding force?
Been that assertive voice
Kept you grounded and given you strength
At times of need
At times when your family has grown and deceased
Who was there for you to keep you complete?
Who have you kept complete?At the age you
currently are
Do you know yourself as you should?
Do you know what you like?
What you're capable of doing
And what you would?

This is food for thought
That questions your decisions
Provokes inner thinking
And promotes the truth
To the forefront of your mind

No more excuses or attempts
To leave unresolved issues behind
Deal with them now
Revaluate your thinking and time
Cry if you need to
And laugh where necessary
But deal with your issues
Then move forward and live your life

Love's Woes
and Joys

I Wish

I wish I could stroll with you
On the beach, through the countryside
Or through the woods kicking autumn leaves
Playfully with you

I wish I could sit back to back with you
And read for a while
Reason and deliberate
On current affairs, literature, entertainment and life

I wish I could mediate and pray with you
In a candle lit scented room
Or have us read scriptures to each other
As I lay head to head with you
Under the presence of the stars and the moon

I wish I could cook with you
Chop, slice and dice with you
Season and marinate
Bake, steam and fry with you
Then set the table for two with you

I wish I could be embraced by you
Be held tightly within your arms
Motionless
Just listening to the beat of your heart
Feeling warm, secure and confident within your calm

Future Poet

I wish we could laugh and cry together
Have misunderstandings and make up together
Feel the hurt by another within each other
Recognise when space is required from each other

I wish I knew who "you" were
The person that can perform the actions within my
words
I wish I knew who "you" were
I wish I knew who "you" were

Black Rose

I am that Black Rose
The one he picked and chose
The rose that smelt sweet to his nose
The rose he held close and chose

I am that Black Rose
The one he loves and knows
The rose from which love flows
The rose whose outer and inner beauty shows

I am that Black Rose
The one he made multiply and grow
The rose that stood firm when hurricanes would blow
The rose that would reap all that he sowed

I am that Black Rose
The one to which others oppose
The rose which makes his aura glow
That rose that spiritually freed his soul

I am that Black Rose

Always on my mind

You're special and you're loveable
You're loyal and you're truthful
Charmingly irresistible
Indescribably admirable and soulful
I become excited at the thought of you
You're reasonable and sensual
In your presence all is possible
Because our love's so real and so visible
It's genuine and it's original
It's what you feel
And what I feel
It's spiritual and it's memorable
It's valuable and it's natural
And it's all the little things you do
Which makes you who I want to share my heart with
And you who I want to chill and vibe with
And you who I want to cry and laugh with
And you who I want to wake up with
Because I'm in love with just loving you
I'm high on love and it's because of you
You're image is the beginning and end of my mind's
spare time
You have my heart fluttering, my pulse racing
And my spirit on cloud nine
You're my soul mate and my best friend
Together, life's ladder I'd like us to climb
Because you are the one
You're who I love
And I know this because…
You are always on my mind

I'm Feeling You

I'm feeling you…
In my mind
And in my thoughts

In between my thighs
I'm feeling your energy
Your presence
Your aura
And your vibe

I'm feeling your breath on my neck
The beat of your heart on my hand
I'm hearing your voice in my head
I'm feeling your nature rise against my leg

I'm feeling the essence of your spirit
The charisma of your psyche
The attractiveness of your finesse
I can feel your hand on my breast
Your love has become my quest

When we embrace…
I can feel the strength of your soul
The eloquent intensity of your passion
I become mesmerised by your physique
I'm feeling the phenomenal force of emotions as our
lips meet

My body's feeling your kisses
It's hypnotised by your touches
As my hands feel the smoothness of your chocolate
skin
I release all of my sexual emotions within

Future Poet

Our sexes finally meet
We become spellbound by our erotic heat
I'm feeling the ecstatic pleasure of your penetration
My sex has become infatuated with this sensation

I'm feeling the rhythm of your heart
The shiver down your spine
Your seductive, stimulating love making
Has totally blown my mind

I'm feeling you as I told you at the start
In my mind
In my thoughts
And in my heart

This exquisite feeling
Has kept my mind racing
Kept my heart beating
And has my love chasing…
You!!!

I love you

I love you
Heaven alone knows what I'd do without you
You are my land and my ocean
You are my sun and my moon
When I'm with you all's kosher
You are my silver spoon
You are the reason for my drive
You are the cause of my smile
You're the love of my life
You're my essence and my style
You can tame me
And drive me wild
You can be the calm in my storm
And the other way round
You can lift me high
And keep my feet on the ground
You are my everything
And to me that is sound

Secret Lover

My lover's a secret
Under my covers his identity is kept
My lover's a secret
After work to my home he crept
My lover's a secret
At times from passion he's overslept
My lover's a secret
Last night his wife wept while she slept
My lover's a secret
Don't assume she's unaware or inept
My lover's a secret
Don't try to understand the concept
My lover's a secret
That's something I've learnt to accept
My lover's a secret
So please don't intercept
My lover's a secret
And it's just the way I like it

The Affair

He shares his time
He shares his grind
He shares the thoughts that lay in his mind
He shares the pain
But doesn't see the crying
He shares himself
Via love and hates thin line
He shares those words
"I love you and all will be fine!"

She gives him her smile
Knowing the truth all the while
She gives him her womanhood
Often feeling used and vile
She gives him her trust
Hoping he will change his life's style
She gives him an inch
He takes an entire mile
She finds the other woman's number
But will she ever dial?

Southern Comfort

I am your wife
Ring or no ring
I've given you my life
I've been your rock
Standing firm by your side
Taken on board your stresses and strife
And now my heart
You wound and cut deep
With pain as your knife
I never knew the cruelty you had in you
I never knew that a perfect love like ours could reign
untrue
So I'm withdrawing the love I had within you
Simply because the you I thought I knew
Just isn't the real you
For too long I've allowed you to dictate
For too long my house has been my prison
With you as the screw and me as the inmate
But now it's time for the tables to rotate
The game's gone on too long
And now it's checkmate
My love for you ran ocean deep
And in return on my trust you cheat
Outside the house you choose to sleep
With her and her you continue to creep
Well take a good look at those bags on the street
The contents are yours
And the keys you can keep
I've changed the locks and put out all the stops
No more tears will my eyes allow to drop
Because I'm celebrating now
With Southern Comfort on the rocks

My Regrets

No matter how I try to explain
Or try and word the situation in a different way
My mistake still remains the same
I can say no more
I know I'm to blame
I want to say 'sorry'
But it seems so cliché
It's like the word 'love'
It means so much and so little
Depending on how or when you say it
But the depth of my regret
Requires more than one word to express
I hurt you, I know
I didn't think, I know
My act was wrong, I know
The sorrow I have hangs my head in shame
And has my spirit low
And I've nothing to show
Other than the pain and anger
That your aura flows
And I don't blame you
Because I am the cause
I've disappointed you
And upset you
But please believe
These words I say are true
From the depth of my soul
The valley's of my mind
The bottom of my heart
And the root of my pride
I regret my wrongdoing and I'm sorry
I should have seen it from your side

Your Words

Your words just aren't enough
To release this grudge
Time has embedded too much hate into this love
I've tried effortlessly to keep
The smooth from being rough
But this time your words just aren't enough
My mental's hardened
And I've become spiritually tough
I've freed my heart
From your restrictive and possessive handcuffs
I've no need to deal with your lies and stuff
I'm off to find true love
Because this time your words just aren't enough
I've had it with you
I've totally had enough
This time your words just aren't enough

Tears on my pillow

What we are doing is senseless
We know what we are feeling within ourselves
And we are completely defenceless
We can't control this
To separate ourselves from each other's lives forever
And stay amicable is ridiculous
Because we are each other's weakness

Things weren't right before
Because we weren't right before
You weren't really you
And I definitely weren't me
We came together with some real unresolved
personal issues
And yeah we tried to plead ignorant to them and ride
through
Not realising that we would be the victims of the
dishonesty to ourselves
Of what we really wanted
What we really needed out of life
For our individual selves
Let alone from each other
And on a reasoning level
We left too much unspoken
As words of real emotion was never our speciality
Other than the usual
And that's because we were all about the connection

Our sprits were irresistibly dancing
Our souls were consciously intertwining
Our hearts were seeking, finding and combining
And our chemistry was making…
Love …just pure love

Future Poet

It's indescribable the way it embodied us
When we'd be in each others presence
Only you and I know that a simple brush of hands
Or unanticipated invasion of personal body space
would skip heart beats
Only you and I know that when we embrace it's…
powerful
Our breaths are taken away
Our hearts beat as one
Words don't come into play
Because we are making love
Gods' way

So how can I depart from that?
How can I leave you and God's way behind?
These words are the woes of my pride
These are my memories of our wordless love's joys
and sorrows
These words are the tears on my pillow

When

A promise is a comfort to a fool
So that must mean that I am the fool of all fools
It must mean that I'm a fool for hoping and believing

Believing in that gift of second chance
Believing that for once his lips had spoken a true
word
Believing that his clarity would be shown in his
actions
And not just faintly heard through mumbled words

I ask myself again …
Have I again succumb to be a victim of my own
kindness
Have I again let my heart's emotions make a fool of
me
Have I again put unnecessary strain on my mental to
create my own unhappiness?
Unfortunately the answer to the above is yes!
I've told him so many times that I no longer want to
know

I've told myself so many times to let him and my
feelings go
And to have no interaction just to let time pass
But again…I don't listen
And once intertwined and the bullshit starts
The same questions arise all over again and to
myself I have to ask ….

Where and when does this episode of kindness and
forgiveness end?
When will love stop being my enemy?

Future Poet

And when will loneliness stop being my friend?
When will comfort embrace me?
When will my happiness be real and not pretend?
When will I be in love and be loved?
When will I find my true special friend?
When will I listen to the wisdom borne out of my
experiences?
When will I move forward?
When?

Again

You have become amicable and attentive
After having breathed…. again
You have exhaled with forgiveness
To put aside feelings of hatred and disappointment
again
You've released all negative emotions
That you once had attached to the thought of your
friend
You were on the road to recovery
Becoming all whole again
But you were emotionally caught off guard too many
times by your friend
And oh shit….
You started to believe again

You let your kind nature run its patient course
You let yourself get caught up
In more than pleasantries and small talk
You tell yourself…"It's cool, I can handle it, I've been
here before!"
Try to convince yourself that this time words spoken
were true, for sure
And you respond to emotions rather than use
common sense
And foolishly you start to believe again

But thankfully your protective instincts rise up within
you again
And you're reminded of the patterns of your friend
You begin to question your mindset
And so you not only seek
But you also find out more about your friend
You have suspicions visually confirmed

Future Poet

And painfully remember why you can do without them
You remember where you are in life
And it's not because of them
But despite them
And as common sense kicks in
You laugh within at the ridiculous thoughts you were
really having
You cry with laughter at the heartache you were
again considering undertaking
All because foolishly you started to believe again

Getting It All Back

I am getting it all back
The look
The confidence
The body and stance
I am getting it all back
All the feelings I used to have…about me
I am getting it all back
The positive mindset
That once told me "failure was not an option"
Has now come back
I am striking that balance between single mum and
single woman
I am getting my social life back
My aspirations back
My entire love for life back
I am getting it all back
No more sad face and lack of motivation
No more excuses of "too tired" and "don't have the
time"
Trust me… I am getting it all back
I've put my right foot forward and my left has
instinctively followed
I'm walking out of this frame of mind that had taken
set
Leaving behind second guessing and all uncertainty
I am on my way to get more from the journey of my
life
As I am the maker of my destiny
My dreams and aspirations have all come back
And I am going to succeed in completing and
achieving all of my goals
Because the I that I know has come back

Changing

I am changing
And removing issues off of my mind
And people out of my life that are draining
And weighing me down
With actions and words that had my smile turned to a
frown

I am changing
I am speaking to God daily
Giving thanks
Asking for forgiveness and praying
Not just for me
But for those around me to also be blessed
And freed
From life's unnecessary stress

I am changing
I now know how to love me
And how I should be loved
I now know what brings me down
And what lifts me up

I am changing
I understand myself better now
I intend to live to my full potential
With less procrastination and distractions around

I am changing
For better not for worse
As I quench my thirst
And drink from the fountain of confidence and self-
worth
To prevent life's stress from manifesting within me

Causing pain and making my body and soul hurt

I am changing
Who and what I choose to love
And give my time and energy to
Or even allow to be in my presence with a negative
vibe
Demeanour or attitude

I am changing
Because I saw and felt the need to
I had held in too much and cried for too long
My mindset and mental picture of life
Was powerfully wrong

I used to look at life through pessimistic eyes
I always thought everyone's life was better than mine
I never put myself first or realised my self-worth
I hadn't been grateful for what I had
I was never satisfied or happy
Just temporarily glad
I lived in my own world that was depressive and sad

That was sometime ago
And I am amazed at how much my life has grown
The decisions I have made
And the way my life's evolved

I am changing because I want to succeed
With the qualities, persona, character and beauty
God has blessed and bestowed upon me
I am changing because I want to be successful in life
By just being me!

Life on a

Serious Note

Our Future, Their History

Is it right to give our children false hope
When as adults, we ourselves can barely cope
If we don't drink
Then some of us smoke
Or we're prescribed pills
Or taking illegal dope
Then we are quick to tell our children
Don't drink, touch weed, pop pills or do coke

Would we be blatantly lying?
When telling our children
All will be fine
When sitting on the surface of our minds
Children their age and size our dying
From the effects of politics and genocide
War, famine and gun crime

Should we tell our western children how thankful they
should be?
When they complain about what's for dinner
Or how pocket money they receive
Innocently unaware of how what they got
Actually came to be
On a low income, breadline salary

Do we always tell our children the truth?
About their tree, their stem and their roots
Or are we too hurt and ignorant about our past
That we never tell them all
We only tell them half
Leaving them like lost souls
Because the memories we have are too deep and
harsh

Future Poet

How is anyone to make a difference within our
society?
When visually on the TV
Is the promotion of sex, drugs, war and poverty
Our children's forefathers shown to be living
In hate, violence and misery

As adults we need to change within ourselves
And stop deluding our children's sanity
We need to start facing up to the flaws
Installed in the man within humanity
What we make of our future
Naturally becomes our children's history
We have to live our lives through ourselves
And not expect our children
To be what we want and should be

All Eyes on Me

There are eyes on me
I know I'm being watched
Someone's breaking down my every move
Listening to my every sound
There are eyes on me
I know I've been clocked
I can't see them
But I can feel them
Whose they are is a mystery to me?

Think about...
Do we really have a private life once we're at home?
Or is the latest technology invading our undisclosed
zone
Are we being watched through our TV's?
Are we being heard through our phones?
Does someone out there know everything I know?
Do they see everything I see?
It's all down to feeling watched why I have this
curiosity

Films that show our future
Are they fake or are they real?
They could be a preview of what the government's
not ready to reveal
Why do film writers and novelists expose us to things
that don't exist?
Why are unusual circumstances always denied and
covered up with government bullshit?

We're all in the system you know
We're all apart of someone's game
Our futures have been planned out whether they lose
or gain

Future Poet

What exactly is the truth and who exactly knows it?
What is it that they have in store for humanity?
And how long will it take before we are wiped out by
new age technology?

Could this be why the rich get richer and the poor get
poorer?
Is this the reason why so many of us suffer?
Someone's watching I know they are
They're watching you as well as me

Our destiny may lie in their lands
But will we allow our fate to lay their hands?

What's the point?

What is the point of a man taking another man's life?
What is the point of a child being killed by a child with a knife?
What was the point of our ancestors fighting for our freedom, dignity & grace?
If we all intend to do is wipe out our entire race.
We're killing our dj's, musicians and politicians.
We're maiming our doctors, lawyers and entrepreneurs.
We're subjecting our children to pain, sorrow, suffering and hurt.
We're living in communities with shootings, stabbings, raping and drug taking.
Why can't we start loving and just stop hating?
We need to drop the ignorance and start using common sense.
We need to put down the guns, the drugs and the violence.
We need to stop the tabloids printing headlines that read....
'Witnesses held in silence"

Ghost

Your blood is pouring like rain
Your tears are falling from pain
The breath from your lungs has drained
Our memories are permanently stained
Yes, another young life has gone down the drain
What was your purpose and your aim?
How long did you think you'd last in this game?
How will you relish in your glory, fortune and fame
Now that the cemetery is where your head is laying
From the guns with which you were once playing
And now you're gone those guns are still spraying
And slaying innocent people
Who were once saying...
"It will never be me "
"I will never die in vain "
But a hospital bed is now where they are staying
And their families have no witnesses and no one to
blame
Other than the gun with which you were once playing

Young Blood

Are you your own leader?
Your own atmosphere creator
A persistent crowd pleaser
The vibe originator
Or the humble unseen gazer

Are you the weakest link?
Intoxicated by the strongest drink
Blinded by every kaleidoscopic blink
Taken…
As you pop that 'E'
Light that pipe
And forget to think

Do you do as your blood tells you to?
And not as you know is true
Or do you do unto others
As you would like them to do unto you

Do you see through your blood's counterfeit
friendship?
Or are you blinded by your own self-consciousness?
Confused by your Blood's realness
Lost in time's temporary stillness
And victimised by your own adolescent pureness

Do you hear the heaviest beat?
Do you write the deepest rhyme?
Do you sing the highest note?
Or commit the grimiest crime
And imprison the prime of your lifetime
For that penny, pound, quarter or dime

Future Poet

Do ladies like you, love you or hate you?
Do you treat them, wine them and dine them?
Or speech them, lean them, bang them, then leave
them?
Do you protect yourself from STD's that could be
breeding?
In the females you are loving, sleeping and
mistreating

Do you value your heartbeat?
As fiercely as your rep on the street
Do you realise your memories will be forever
bittersweet?
Living by your Blood's rules
No surrender, no retreat

Young Blood take charge
You were born unique
When necessary learn to turn the other cheek
Be concerned if you have footsteps that follow in your
feet
Ensure… your mistakes
They…don't repeat

And if in life's race you wish to compete
Remember rule number one
Learn to think with your own head
And lead your own feet

Black Woman

Are you weaved and styled
Or relaxed and dyed
Maybe even natural with locs or braided
And remained as God intended

Or do you bleach your skin
Thinking the lighter you are
The easier you'll fit in
With the image the world
Projects of us as Black Women

Are you a roots girl or a soul sister?
The city chick who's a big spender
Maybe even a hardworking single baby mother

Do you have every schoolgirl's perfect dream?
The kids, the house, the car
And a man who does what he says
And says what he means

Or are you unhappy with your choice
And can't stand when he raises his voice
Then the blows start to rain
Leaving you feeling helpless, terrified
Crying and in pain

Then days later he's back
Saying sorry again
Would you say you are an independent
Confident Black woman
Who strives for what she wants
Regardless of the challenge
And holds her head high

Future Poet

Because she knows she has
Flare, personality and talent

Do you live your life for you?
Or to how others think you should
And in turn
You're trapped by the stress they give
You try to keep the peace
Because a stress free and humble life
Is the kind of life you wish to live

When you look in the mirror
Do you like what you see?
Or are you unhappy with your external representative
And how your personality and inner-self is being
projected
To the eyes of those around you
Those that love you, hate you
And don't even know you

Whatever type of woman you feel you are
Remember if you stay spiritually strong, ambitious and
true to yourself
You'll be destined to go far
Let no one take away your self's natural being
Because you were created by God
To be a beautiful, genuine, unique Black Woman

Black Warriors

No more can I stand to see
Black warriors falling like leaves
From the branches of life's autumn trees
Part of me just refuses to believe
They've lost their bond
The connection of their conception
The reason why they were conceived
Through time's course it seems
They've subconsciously detached their souls from
their inherited inner peace and essence
Some have chosen to live amongst Babylon as
thieves, murders and peasants
Even though history tells us
The world would not be
If not for our ingenious presence
"Western life is hard!" Some warriors cry
"There's just no other way!"
Simply because that's what Babylon has shown them
and told them
So that is what they will say
But every man, woman and child was born with an
inner voice
And when they hear it
If they listen or not
Is really their choice
But if we, as a people, are to continue to rise from
slavery's
Deaths, chains, rapes and beatings
Then we need to drop Babylon's demoralising
teachings
We need to know our history from its highest heights
To its deepest dwellings
We need to remember *we are*

Future Poet

Not was, inventors
Of some of the world's greatest things
We need to study and take heed of our ancestor's teachings
Adopt them and intertwine them with how we are now living
Right now Babylon's people have nothing they need to claim
Centuries have passed and they are still playing the same game
They've prepared and planned
To mentally weaken and drain
The pride, dignity, courage and strength that flows through our warriors veins
Imagine, we are years into the millennium
And many warriors still don't know their last name
So how can they know where they are going
If they have no idea where they came from
Living under Babylon's reign
Will only make our warriors weak, not strong
That's why '**acknowledgement of self'**
Is what we need to teach our youths
Because the whole of the world's history stems from the Black Warriors roots

Sister

For him you gave birth
So naturally your love for him will come first
You're the woman that quenches his thirst
Relaxes his mind
Makes him feel superior and fine
You've helped to make him excel and shine
Yet when he crosses that thin line between love and hate
And starts to become your enemy instead of your mate
You allow him to think its okay
You allow him to treat your temple in the wrong way
You allow him to think "sorry" is all he has to say
Because tomorrow he'll be a better man
Because tomorrow is a new day
But you know and I know
Tomorrow will be the same

The same voice that whispered sweet nothings in your ear
Will be used as a weapon to have you frozen with fear
And the same hands that undress you, touch you, feel you and caress you
Will hit you, punch you, beat you and mistreat you
The same dick that pleases you and teases you
Will forcefully penetrate you and rape you

And the same man that needs you, wants you, adores you and completes you
Will dislike you, hate you, despise you and will want to see your demise

Future Poet

While tears fall from your children's eyes
They're hearing your screams of terror
Feeling the pain from your cries
How much more can Mummy endure
Daddy please don't hit Mummy no more
In your home you should feel secure
Not hiding behind a locked bathroom door

Sister this mister's not for you
I've told you a million times before
His words of "I love you" are untrue to the meaning
taken by me and you
There's no love without pain
But love doesn't condone blows that rain
Love doesn't hurt you because you complain
Love doesn't desert you and tell you you're to blame
In love you should not lose
You should only gain

Sister this mister's not for you
I'm sorry to say
But love just doesn't hurt you and treat you in this
way

The Rising of our Falling

How many of us are at the bottom of the sea
Dead bodies thrown overboard
Their battered souls finally free
No more beatings, no more chains
No more hurting from human on human
Barbaric merciless mistreating
That was once our ancestor's way of life
Under the restraints of slavery's strife
And yet they struggled
And held their head high
Their strength released their spirit
Which allowed their souls to fly
And they survived
They made a stand in numbers
And fought for their rights
They freed their lives
Which is how we eventually came to rise

But now with years lived
We are falling from the makings of our own demise
Tear's our mother's cry
While undertaker's smile, as their profits rise
Society sighs, stereotypes form
All black youths are wild

That is not the case
If the truth be known
Their identity seems to be misplaced
They give up too easy
Can't be bothered with the chase
Tired of being misjudged
By the race of their face
Forgetting that tune has been over played

Future Poet

Because if there is the will
Then there always is a way

You see it's the contents of their minds
That needs to be underlined
It's what they view with their own eyes
At home in their private lives
Away from the world's eyes
Not too mention the other sights
On the box of tell-lie-vision
That comes from a cable or via the sky

Our children are having children
And becoming confused by their quick rush of life
Wanting to be as old as they look
Before they are mentally wise
Too eager to make it on their own
Regardless of wrong or right
Then turning to a hustler's life of grime
Becoming a gun owner or victim of its crime
A drug dealer or user
Constantly trying to get high

As adults we need not criticise, but sympathise
'Fore they are not like us, their culture is westernised
It's guidance that they seek
To change the course of their lives
And not all our youths are bad
So I won't generalise
But we need to come together as one
To stop our people from dying
We've buried too many in too little time
And we've made it this far down our ancestry line
With our own businesses and such
And hopes and dreams that come alive

We can help to better another person's way of life
Give some moral support, a few words of friendly
advice
It's what we need to do if our race is to ever survive
We need to show more love for each other
To eradicate the rise in our demise

For the world

The position I've been placed in
Has caused the actions I've created
Life is short, time is precious
I don't believe that they should be wasted
I have been placed here, on this earth
Like you, to experience all I already know
I'm here to reap the benefits from the seeds of love
That I have and will continue to sow

I long to be happy and content
Without troubles, insecurities and woe
I strive to allow my talents, strengths and passions to
glow
I strive to have longevity
And for only joy and goodness for my future to behold
But the times we are living in are uncertain
And so before I go

I am preparing for my life's experiences
And my learned knowledge to be known and shown
By all whose presence has intertwined with mine
By all those who I'll never meet not once in this
lifetime
And by those who have faith and belief
In the power of their spiritual mind
And by those who dwell in iniquities
And live unrighteous to mankind

The position I've been placed in
Has led to my cries before my demise
That mankind will one day live hand in hand
No poverty, no famine, no wars, no fights
Just man, woman and child

Living together for one another
In one peace, God's love and one vibe
To see this world, our world, God's world
Live harmoniously as one
Will make me cherish everyday I live before I die

Credits

This book cover was designed by Mansor Sy, a specialist in architecture and graphic design. For more information contact Mansor Sy at:

msooresy@aol.com

Other Businesses of Interest

Future Poet

Future Poet specialises in personalised framed poetry, greeting cards and spoken word performances. If you are interested in these services you can contact Future Poet at:

msfuturepoet@hotmail.com or visit www. myspace.com/futurepoetswords

Studio Six Nine

Studio Six Nine is a recording studio which offers facilities for digital recording, live recording and mastering. For further information visit:

www.studiosixnine.com or www.myspace.com/ studiosixnine

The Freedom Initiative

The Freedom Initiative facilitates behavioural and crime intervention workshops and also delivers diversity and personal development training. These crime prevention services are specifically aimed at 13-19 year olds who have behavioural problems and may be considered hard to reach or at risk of offending.

For further information visit: www. thefreedominitivative.co.uk

The Bridge

The Bridge is an innovative and interactive new youth politics show and it provides an interactive platform to create new ways of encouraging young people to participate in Politics and TV. The Bridge aims to enlighten, educate and empower young people to campaign and take action in their communities and the wider world.

For further information visit: www.thebridgeuk. co.uk

Or send an email to: Chris@thebridgeuk.co.uk

LL Coaching

Life coaching inspires and motivates you to achieve your dreams and reach your full potential, creating a life that is full of balance and fulfillment.

For further information visit: www.llcoaching.co.uk

Or send an email to: leanne@llcoaching.co.uk

Success University

Success University provides online personal development and gives you access to the world's leading Personal Development Experts. So if you love personal development and want to fulfill your potential visit:

www.teamturbosu.com or www.youwork4you.successuniversity.com

E-Creative (Escapism Group)

E-Creative designs and prints all business stationary and merchandise to suit your requirements.

For further information contact: info@escapismgroup.co.uk